SIMPLY
TAROT

*Unlock the mysteries
of tarot and discover
what lies ahead*

HB

HINKLER
BOOKS

Author: Amanda Hall
Art Director: Karen Moores
Editor: Jane Keighley & Margaret Barca
Graphic Artist: Melissa Carroll
Packaging and Cover Design: Michael Raz
Tarot Card Photography: A.A. Photography
Tarot Card Image Design: Merlin Digital Art
Assistant Co-ordinator: Jack Egerton
Photo credits: Dreamland © Leeloomultipass/Dreamstime.com;
Celestial Sun Ornament © Patricia Legg/istockphoto.com
Special thanks to Michele Slik

Published by Hinkler Books Pty Ltd
45-55 Fairchild Street
Heatherton, VIC 3202 Australia
www.hinklerbooks.com

Text © Hinkler Books Pty Ltd 2005
Packaging and Cover Design © Hinkler Books Pty Ltd 2009

Printed and bound in China

2 4 6 8 10 9 7 5 3
10 12 14 13 11

ISBN 978 1 7418 4511 2

CONTENTS

INTRODUCTION

Tarot cards have been used for many centuries to help guide people in their lives and to help them understand the emotional issues influencing their lives. Tarot can be used to bring insight and understanding to personal and professional situations. Working with the Tarot regularly can help you to be aware of changes in your life and to use opportunities for the better. The Tarot is a form of fortune-telling or predicting events. The correct term is divination.

You do not need any special skill to work with the Tarot, but you need to have an open mind and allow the cards to form a story in the way they are laid. A reading of the cards will give answers and advise on how to handle and approach your life. When I perform a reading for my clients, I ask them to shuffle the cards on the table to commence the reading. A reading is different for each person, as everyone has unique and varied problems and lessons in their journey of life. The cards work on a very personal and emotional level, tapping into your higher self or subconscious mind. The cards bring out the positive and negative aspects surrounding you.

When I do a reading I do not ask a question, but allow the cards to describe the answers needed. The Tarot may not always give the answers you expect, but will give you the information needed to look at the issues from an angle you may not have considered. However, you still have free-will and are able to control your own thoughts and actions. I believe that forewarned is forearmed and the Tarot can help us make more informed choices to enrich our lives.

HISTORY & ORIGIN OF THE TAROT

No one really knows where the Tarot had its origins, but the history of the Tarot cards in Europe seems to date back to the 14th century – to the days of Marco Polo. The original teaching of the Tarot is said to be based on 22 pewter plates, which made up the Major Arcana. A reading of these was used to decide when to plant crops, or to make decisions for a nation such as when to go to war.

Many years later the Minor Arcana cards were added to the Tarot. The Minor Arcana consists of 56 cards, which are the basis of the playing deck we use today for card games. In the Minor Arcana we also include four more court cards called the Pages. Images on the cards are used to help understand and perform readings with the Tarot.

Although many countries claim to have introduced the Minor Arcana, my personal belief is that the Romany gypsies of northern Europe introduced these cards to the Tarot. Throughout history the gypsies have been known for their fortune-telling skills and ability to predict the future.

This may be where the myth comes from that you cannot buy your own Tarot cards. The Romany gypsies had a tradition that, when the grandmother of the group was to retire, she would pass her tools of trade on to her eldest granddaughter. Thus the wisdom and knowledge of the Tarot would pass from one generation to the next.

There are many myths about the Tarot which have evolved through time. Some believe that the Tarot deck is very personal to the owner and should not be touched by another person. This choice remains in your hands. However I always ask my client to shuffle the cards before a reading commences.

Another myth says that before using your cards you need to sleep with them under your pillow for up to a week, to personally energise them. I have found no logical reason or improvement in the ability to read cards from following this practice. It has also been said that after wrapping your cards in a purple silk scarf for protection and safe-keeping from evil spirits and unwanted energies, they should be placed in a wooden box and only used on a wooden table.

Tarot is an extremely individual practice and belief that needs to be treated with respect for its ancient wisdom. You should allow your own feelings and desires about how and when you will perform a reading. You may like to choose a place where you believe your own personal energy is strongest and only perform readings in that particular place. You may wish to incorporate a tablecloth of your choice and burn a candle or incense to create a peaceful mood that enhances the experience for you and the person you are performing the reading for. This is a personal choice and is not essential to performing a Tarot reading. The main ingredient is a relaxed environment, where you feel at peace with yourself. Allow plenty of time to ponder the message the cards are sharing with you.

There have been many changes over time. For example, there was no reversed meaning in the original teaching of the Tarot beliefs. This was only added in the 19th century. I personally do not believe in reversed meanings, as this was only introduced to make changes to the Tarot for copyright issues in the 19th century. The meaning does not change because it is upside down or reversed.

READING THE TAROT

Before you begin to do a reading you need to clear your mind of all thoughts. Shuffle the deck, then take the cards from the top of the deck (unless otherwise instructed) and place them on the table, working from left to right. The Tarot cards all have meanings, and the meanings need to be considered in relation to where they fall in a 'spread'. The position in which a card falls helps to clarify the message of the Tarot.

The significator, or querent as it was known in the earlier teaching of the Tarot, is the person you are performing the reading for. The card chosen to represent the significator can be decided by the sex, age, hair and eye colouring of the person. Choosing the significator card is used in many Tarot spreads as a point of focus or starting point of a reading. For example, if the significator or querent is a woman over 25 years of age with fair hair and blue eyes, we would choose the Queen of Cups. If the female is under 25 years of age we would choose the Page of Cups.

When you commence studying the Tarot, it is advisable to learn the meanings of each card. You need to become familiar with the images and take time to practise.

Later, when you become more experienced, you will be able to use your own intuitive abilities to enhance your reading.

The *Simply Tarot* Deck has been designed with simplicity in mind, which will allow the student to absorb and quickly learn the basic meanings of the Tarot cards. These meanings are printed on the bottom of the cards as a guide, to enable the person performing the reading to add their own interpretation.

Anyone can have a reading, but it is always easier to read for someone who has an open mind and will be receptive to the information being given. People may not always get the answers they expect, and may not want to believe the answers given, but I have never found the cards to be wrong. We still have the right to make our own choices. People still retain the free will to control their destiny.

When you commence your journey into the study of the Tarot, you may like to keep your readings in a special journal or notebook for future reference. I suggest a hardcover book with ruled lines so you can record the following information:

• Date of reading
• Question in your mind
• The cards and Tarot spread used
• Your findings of the reading and how you felt emotionally at the time of the reading
• Other notes at the time of the reading for your future reference

This will enable you to chart the progress achieved in your life due to the guidance and wisdom of the Tarot cards.

THE CARDS

The Tarot consists of 78 cards in all. The Major Arcana has 22 cards, numbered from 0 to 21, each with a symbolic image. The cards are said to tell a story – the journey of life – with the figures and symbols representing different characteristics and experiences in life.

The Minor Arcana has 56 cards, divided into four suits – Cups, Wands, Swords and Pentacles. Each suit is numbered from Ace to 10 and also has four court cards – Page, Knight, Queen and King.

The *Simply Tarot* Deck was created by understanding the need to bring the Tarot message into the 21st century. With particular attention to detail and conveying all the right symbology and hidden imagery of the Rider Waite Deck, many hours were spent perfecting each card. The *Simply Tarot* Deck blends the mystique of the original Rider Waite Deck, using real imagery instead of drawings. We have also included the basic meanings on the card to help enhance and simplify the learning process for the student. The colour and detail make them a very special set of cards with much information to share.

In the history of the Tarot and other psychic-related subjects, there are unspoken rules and guidelines which have become uniform around the world and have been used for centuries.

In this book we will be using the *Simply Tarot* Deck. Some decks on the market have quite grotesque drawings which may frighten people. Tarot cards have taken on many different styles featuring mythology, cats, female energy, fairies and the inner child, to name a few. When choosing a set of cards, you need to be comfortable with the drawings and colours. For beginners, I believe you can't go wrong if you choose the *Simply Tarot* Deck.

CUPS

WANDS   *SWORDS*

PENTACLES

THE BACK OF THE CARDS

The sun placed in the top right corner of the card symbolises the male, or ego, energy, which always relates to the right-hand side of the body. The sun is always seen in the heavens higher than the moon.

The moon is placed towards the bottom of the card on the left to symbolise the female, or the subjective, psychic energy, which always relates to the left-hand side of the body and is always lower in the heavens than the sun.

The stars are placed in the surrounding sky to represent the heavens and all the knowledge and light to be shared with both male and female.

PSYCHIC PROTECTION

Before you work with the Tarot cards you need to protect yourself against the wrong information being given to you by the spirit guides.

WHAT IS A SPIRIT GUIDE?

A spirit guide is chosen to guide and protect you on your earth journey. My personal belief is that a spirit guide is a family member who has passed over to the other side and who decides, for a number of reasons, to protect and guide you throughout your life. There may be many different reasons why they choose you rather than another member of your family. They may a feel a close affinity with you because you remind them of their personality and have a similar belief system to them. They may like the way you conduct your life and feel their skills can help you achieve more of your ambitions. The reasons are diverse and differ in each individual situation. We may not have personally known them before they passed over to the other side.

Now we need to learn how to perform psychic protection.

Close your eyes and imagine yourself in some form of gold. It could be a triangle, a coat, under a golden shower of rain, in a car or anything meaningful to you. Or you may just like to hold a gold cross in your hand. This only takes a couple of seconds and should be carried out before you commence every reading.

TAROT SPREADS

Many different card spreads have been designed over the years, but the spread that has become most widely used around the world is the Celtic Cross. This informs us about the issues surrounding us at the present moment, the influences from the past or influences that are leaving our lives, the events coming into our lives, personal issues, work and home life issues, hopes and fears, or the issues that may be holding us back.

WHICH SPREAD TO CHOOSE

The Mark & Amanda spread is for direct or specific situations or the influences preventing us from resolving a matter. If you need an answer to a direct question use the Mark & Amanda spread. If you feel you need a more in-depth reading, then the Celtic Cross is the spread to choose. Many people use the Celtic Cross spread constantly.

Daily readings can be done with the Daily Inspiration spread, which will help enlighten you about issues surrounding you on that day. Over the years, many spreads have been designed or adapted from other sources of fortune-telling. You will be able to use any spread you find from another source with these cards and be able to perform readings. We all end up with a favourite or two.

THE MAJOR ARCANA

The Major Arcana are the first 22 cards of the deck. They are known as the nouns in the sentence, or the solid part of the reading. They are very powerful in their own right and readings can be done using just these cards.

1 THE MAGICIAN
Element of surprise.
Good or bad.

2 THE HIGH PRIESTESS
Highest card in the Tarot deck.
Very powerful.
Good or bad secrets to be revealed.

These are some interpretations of the Major Arcana cards, which I have found work consistently for me.

THE EMPRESS

Delays will prove necessary.

THE EMPEROR

Stability or stabilising influence coming into your life.

3 THE EMPRESS

Delays will prove necessary.

4 THE EMPEROR

Stability or stabilising influence coming into your life.

THE HEIROPHANT
Marriage. Government or
public company. Body corporate.
Official building or official situation.

THE LOVERS
Love affairs. Romance building again within
marriage. Relationship. Relatives. Loving
relationship you could share with a friend.

5 THE HIEROPHANT

Marriage. Government or public company.
Body corporate. Official building or
official situation.

6 THE LOVERS

Love affairs. Romance building again within
marriage. Relationship. Relatives. Loving
relationship you could share with a friend.

7 THE CHARIOT

7 THE CHARIOT
Movement of residence. Journey.
Victory over a situation or problem.
Balancing the opposite polarities.

8 STRENGTH

8 STRENGTH
Inner strength. Confrontation
with yourself or other people.

THE MAJOR ARCANA *(continued)*

THE HERMIT
Loneliness. Unattached.
Soul-searching time needed
or time alone.

WHEEL OF FORTUNE
Elevation of money. Overseas trip.
Completion phases.

9 THE HERMIT
Loneliness. Unattached.
Soul-searching time needed
or time alone.

10 WHEEL OF FORTUNE
Elevation of money. Overseas trip.
Completion phases.

JUSTICE

Legal situation or document. Police.
Finding out the truth in the matter
affecting the balance.

THE HANGED MAN

Getting stronger in oneself
after a lot of deliberating and
delaying in your life.

11 JUSTICE

Legal situation or document. Police.
Finding out the truth in the matter
affecting the balance.

12 THE HANGED MAN

Getting stronger in oneself
after a lot of deliberating and
delaying in your life.

DEATH

Death of situation or endings.
New beginnings.

TEMPERANCE

Money restrictions.
Testing the waters.

13 DEATH

Death of situation or endings.
New beginnings.

14 TEMPERANCE

Money restrictions.
Testing the waters.

THE DEVIL

*Jealousy or trouble. Able to break
the chains that are binding you
or holding you back.*

THE TOWER

*Catastrophe. Accident.
Things happening very quickly, at
lightning pace.*

15 THE DEVIL

Jealousy or trouble. Able to break
the chains that are binding you
or holding you back.

16 THE TOWER

Catastrophe. Accident.
Things happening very quickly,
at lightning pace.

THE MAJOR ARCANA *(continued)*

THE STAR
Brightness. Hope.
Could bring excesses, so be careful not
to become too greedy.

THE MOON
Deception or delays. Emotions up or down.
May be deceiving yourself
emotionally, or others.

17 THE STAR

Brightness. Hope.
Could bring excesses, so be careful not
to become too greedy.

18 THE MOON

Deception or delays. Emotions up or down.
May be deceiving yourself
emotionally, or others.

THE SUN

Marriage.
Happiness and bright prospects.

JUDGEMENT

Decisions pending finality.
The only decision that can be made
under the circumstances.

19 THE SUN

Marriage.
Happiness and bright prospects.

20 JUDGEMENT

Decisions pending finality.
The only decision that can be made
under the circumstances.

THE WORLD
Overseas trip. Money. Luck.
World in the palm of your hand.
New opportunities.

THE FOOL
Good friends. Happiness.
Needing to take a giant leap forward.

21 THE WORLD

Overseas trip. Money. Luck.
World in the palm of your hand.
New opportunities.

0 THE FOOL

Good friends. Happiness.
Needing to take a giant leap forward.

MARK & AMANDA SPREAD

MAJOR ARCANA ONLY

You would use this spread when you need a direct yes or no answer. Please be aware, however, that if the cards feel there are other issues that need to be addressed, this will be reflected in the cards that come out in the reading. The spread spans a three-month period. It uses cards of the Major Arcana only.

1	2	3	4	5	6	13	14

7	8	9	10	11	12	15	16

ASKING YOUR QUESTION

1 Separate the Major Arcana cards from the deck, then shuffle the cards and ask your question out loud.

2 Take the first six cards from the top of the deck and place face up, in a line, across the table from left to right.

3 Turn the deck over and take the next six cards from the bottom and place face up, in a line, across the table directly underneath the first six cards.

4 If there is no conclusive answer, an extension is required. You proceed in the same manner taking the first two cards from the top and the next two from the bottom of the deck. Place them next to the final outcome (cards 5–6–11–12).

A Sample Reading
Mary's Mark & Amanda Reading

First four cards (1–2–7–8) Relate to the past, or what is just passing.

Middle four cards (3–4–9–10) Relate to the present conditions, or the next situation to follow.

Final four cards (5–6–11–12) Reveal the outcome or to where the situation is leading.

(Cards 13-14-15-16) **The extension is only used when the answer was not clear.**

Question: Should Mary change her job?

Answer:

PAST

In Mary's past, or what is just passing
The Hanged Man, Strength, Justice, The World

Mary has become a lot stronger after a lot of deliberating and delaying surrounding important issues in her life. She has the inner strength to confront herself and the issues. She now has the strength to face the truth about the issues that have been troubling her and this will bring her life into balance. The world is in the palm of her hand. New opportunities for improvements with money, signing of a contract or new agreements will improve her finances greatly.

 1 2
 7 8

PRESENT

The event Mary is facing now
The Sun, The Tower, The Hermit, Wheel of Fortune

Happiness with a lot of bright prospects, even though there has been an end to her marriage. Situations in her life are moving very quickly. Mary has done all her soul-searching and feels she must now move ahead alone with her own opportunities. There have been completion phases in her life and she is moving forward to bring more money into her life.

 3 4
 9 10

FUTURE

The events Mary is facing in the future
The Chariot, The Magician, The Moon, Temperance

Mary will be taking a journey which will bring a major victory into her life. Every issue in her life is moving very quickly and there may also be some surprising situations. Emotions at this time will be very mixed with highs and lows, and there will be some money issues to deal with. This may well be new territory for Mary and she is still testing the waters in her new direction.

 5 6
 11 12

EXTENSION

Extension of Mary's outcome
The Lovers, The Fool, Judgement, The Emperor

Mary is experiencing a lot of loving energy around her at present. With the very strong opportunity for a new romance, she would need to take a giant leap forward with the help of her friends. The decisions Mary is making at the present time are final and the only decisions that could be made under the circumstances. This will bring stability into her life.

 13 14

THE MINOR ARCANA

The Minor Arcana are the remaining 56 cards in the deck, which can be considered the adjectives in the sentence. These cards give more detail and direction with a reading. The four suits of the Minor Arcana are Cups, Wands, Swords and Pentacles.

 ## CUPS (EMOTIONS - HEARTS)
Cups represent people with blue or grey eyes, and fair to light brown hair. Soft, gentle people.

ACE OF CUPS
Security. Helping hand.

2 OF CUPS
Peace of mind.
Joining of two people.

There are key words associated with each suit and interpretations associated with each card. Each of the suits is related to one of the houses in a modern deck of playing cards. For example, Cups relate to the Hearts of a modern playing deck.

3 OF CUPS
Celebration.
Bright happenings.

4 OF CUPS
Money fluctuations. Being offered
something you may not want.

3 OF CUPS
Celebration.
Bright happenings.

4 OF CUPS
Money fluctuations. Being offered
something you may not want.

THE MINOR ARCANA - CUPS *(continued)*

5 OF CUPS
*Money losses. All is not lost,
if you look behind. You may have
something to salvage.*

6 OF CUPS
*Happy house.
Childhood memories.*

5 OF CUPS

Money losses. All is not lost,
if you look behind. You may have
something to salvage.

6 OF CUPS

Happy house.
Childhood memories.

7 OF CUPS

All that glitters is not gold. Look beyond the clouds. Money improvements.

8 OF CUPS

Money problems. Turning your back and walking away, knowing nothing more can be done.

7 OF CUPS

All that glitters is not gold. Look beyond the clouds. Money improvements.

8 OF CUPS

Money problems. Turning your back and walking away, knowing nothing more can be done.

The Minor Arcana - Cups *(continued)*

9 OF CUPS

Improvements underway.
Feeling smug or pleased.

10 OF CUPS

Happiness. Good things.
Party or celebration.

9 OF CUPS

Improvements underway.
Feeling smug or pleased.

10 OF CUPS

Happiness. Good things.
Party or celebration.

PAGE OF CUPS

Young woman to 25 years.
Basic good news.

KNIGHT OF CUPS

Young man to 25 years.
Needing more confidence.

PAGE OF CUPS
Young woman to 25 years.
Basic good news.

KNIGHT OF CUPS
Young man to 25 years.
Needing more confidence.

THE MINOR ARCANA - CUPS *(continued)*

QUEEN OF CUPS
Woman over 25 years.
Blue eyes, fair or brown hair.
Soft, gentle, motherly.

KING OF CUPS
Man over 25 years.
Blue eyes, fair or brown hair.
Gentle, emotional, shy.

QUEEN OF CUPS

Woman over 25 years. Blue eyes, fair or brown hair. Soft, gentle, motherly.

KING OF CUPS

Man over 25 years. Blue eyes, fair or brown hair. Gentle, emotional, shy.

WANDS (ACTION - DIAMONDS)

Wands represent people with green eyes or with flecks of hazel in their eyes, and blonde or red to light brown hair. Positive, motivated people.

ACE OF WANDS
New beginnings. Birth.
New ideas. Creation.

2 OF WANDS
Short journey.
Movement to or near water.

ACE OF WANDS
New beginnings. Birth.
New ideas. Creation.

2 OF WANDS
Short journey.
Movement to or near water.

THE MINOR ARCANA -
WANDS *(continued)*

3 OF WANDS
Travel overland.
Surveying your kingdom.

4 OF WANDS
Happy home.
Possible country setting.

5 OF WANDS

Arguments.
Battles around you.

6 OF WANDS

Letter or news coming.
Victory news.

5 OF WANDS

Arguments.
Battles around you.

6 OF WANDS

Letter or news coming.
Victory news.

The Minor Arcana - Wands *(continued)*

7 OF WANDS

Frustrations. You are able to overcome your frustration. You are on top of the situation.

8 OF WANDS

Speedy news or situation coming. Arrows of love.

7 OF WANDS

Frustrations. You are able to overcome your frustration. You are on top of the situation.

8 OF WANDS

Speedy news or situation coming. Arrows of love.

9 OF WANDS
Undecided.
Need to take a step out of the situation,
then you will see more clearly.

10 OF WANDS
Weighed down with problems.
Very heavy load.

9 OF WANDS

Undecided.
Need to take a step out of the situation.
then you will see more clearly.

10 OF WANDS

Weighed down with problems.
Very heavy load.

THE MINOR ARCANA -
WANDS *(continued)*

PAGE OF WANDS
Young woman to 25 years.
Travel overland.

KNIGHT OF WANDS
Young man to 25 years.
Important letter.

PAGE OF WANDS
Young woman to 25 years.
Travel overland.

KNIGHT OF WANDS
Young man to 25 years.
Important letter.

QUEEN OF WANDS
Woman over 25 years.
Green eyes, blonde to red hair.
Positive, fiery outspoken.

KING OF WANDS
Man over 25 years.
Green eyes, blonde to red hair.
Restless, outspoken, ambitious.

SWORDS (CHALLENGE - SPADES)

Swords represent people with hazel or brown eyes, and brown hair, or grey or greying hair. People whose opinion we respect, not always older people, but those with a reserved and mature outlook.

ACE OF SWORDS
Frustrations. Double-edged sword.
Hollow victory.

2 OF SWORDS
Peace and harmony.
Needing to take the blindfold off.
Keep reassessing the situation at hand.

ACE OF SWORDS
Frustrations. Double-edged sword.
Hollow victory.

2 OF SWORDS
Peace and harmony.
Needing to take the blindfold off.
Keep reassessing the situation at hand.

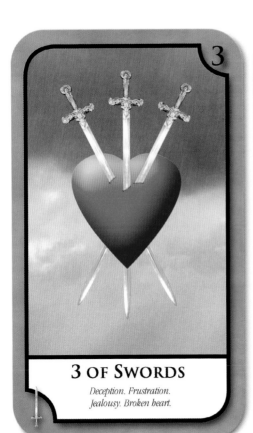

3 OF SWORDS

Deception. Frustration.
Jealousy. Broken heart.

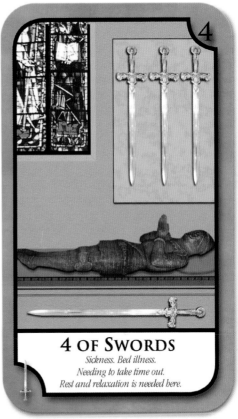

4 OF SWORDS

Sickness. Bed illness.
Needing to take time out.
Rest and relaxation is needed here.

3 OF SWORDS
Deception. Frustration.
Jealousy. Broken heart.

4 OF SWORDS
Sickness. Bed illness.
Needing to take time out.
Rest and relaxation is needed here.

THE MINOR ARCANA - SWORDS *(continued)*

5 OF SWORDS
Losses. All is not lost as
you still have three swords remaining,
giving you the upper hand.

6 OF SWORDS
Boat or over-water travel.
Turning boat out of troubled waters
into calmer waters.

5 OF SWORDS
Losses. All is not lost as
you still have three swords remaining,
giving you the upper hand.

6 OF SWORDS
Boat or over-water travel.
Turning boat out of troubled waters
into calmer waters.

7 OF SWORDS
Plans. Hopes. Wish card.
Highest Minor Arcana.

8 OF SWORDS
Frustrations.
Feeling bound and gagged.

7 OF SWORDS
Plans. Hopes. Wish card.
Highest Minor Arcana.

8 OF SWORDS
Frustrations.
Feeling bound and gagged.

THE MINOR ARCANA -
SWORDS *(continued)*

9 OF SWORDS
Tears and frustrations.
Letting go of emotions.

10 OF SWORDS
Death or ending of situation
or relationship.

9 OF SWORDS
Tears and frustrations.
Letting go of emotions.

10 OF SWORDS
Death or the ending of a situation
or relationship.

PAGE OF SWORDS
Young woman to 25 years.
Spying or deception. Reflecting
back over your shoulder.

KNIGHT OF SWORDS
Young man to 25 years.
Speedy situation or finish.

PAGE OF SWORDS
Young woman to 25 years.
Spying or deception. Reflecting
back over your shoulder.

KNIGHT OF SWORDS
Young man to 25 years.
Speedy situation or finish.

The Minor Arcana - Swords *(continued)*

QUEEN OF SWORDS
Woman over 25 years.
Brown eyes and brown hair.
Cold, hard, demanding authority.

KING OF SWORDS
Man over 25 years.
Brown eyes and brown hair.
Cold, abrasive, demands respect.

QUEEN OF SWORDS

Woman over 25 years.
Brown eyes and brown hair.
Cold, hard, demanding authority.

KING OF SWORDS

Man over 25 years.
Brown eyes and brown hair.
Cold abrasive, demands respect

PENTACLES (MONEY - CLUBS)

Pentacles represent people with brown to black eyes, dark brown to black hair and olive to dark skin tone. Professional or business people.

ACE OF PENTACLES
Money coming.
Divine wish being granted.

2 OF PENTACLES
Money confusion. Juggling two
situations or ideas around.

ACE OF PENTACLES

Money coming.
Divine wish being granted.

2 OF PENTACLES

Money confusion. Juggling two
situations or ideas around.

THE MINOR ARCANA - PENTACLES *(continued)*

3 OF PENTACLES
Improvements under way, but delays around it. Renown, glory. Place of worship.

4 OF PENTACLES
Money improvements. More coming your way.

3 OF PENTACLES
Improvements under way,
but delays around it. Renown, glory.
Place of worship.

4 OF PENTACLES
Money improvements.
More coming your way.

5 OF PENTACLES
Delays around money.
Coming in from the cold.

6 OF PENTACLES
Raise in money or salary.

5 OF PENTACLES
Delays around money.
Coming in from the cold.

6 OF PENTACLES
Raise in money or salary.

The Minor Arcana - Pentacles *(continued)*

7 OF PENTACLES
Work frustrations.
Hard work needing to be done,
either at work or a situation in life.

8 OF PENTACLES
Work, paid work.

7 OF PENTACLES

Work frustrations.
Hard work needing to be done,
either at work or a situation in life.

8 OF PENTACLES

Work, paid work.

9 OF PENTACLES
Peace of mind. Contentment.

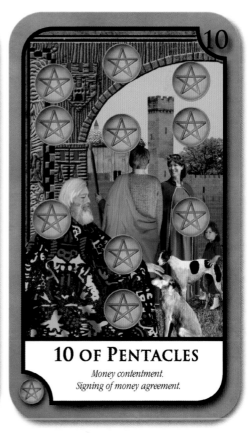

10 OF PENTACLES
Money contentment.
Signing of money agreement.

9 OF PENTACLES
Peace of mind. Contentment.

10 OF PENTACLES
Money contentment.
Signing of money agreement.

Page of Pentacles
Young woman to 25 years.
Student. Male or female.

Knight of Pentacles
Young man to 25 years.
Visitors. Message to share.

QUEEN OF PENTACLES
Woman over 25 years.
Dark eyes and dark hair.
Professional, business, domineering.

KING OF PENTACLES
Man over 25 years.
Dark eyes and dark hair.
Business, arrogance, powerful.

QUEEN OF PENTACLES

Woman over 25 years.
Dark eyes and dark hair.
Professional, business, domineering.

KING OF PENTACLES

Man over 25 years.
Dark eyes and dark hair.
Business, arrogant, powerful.

CELTIC CROSS SPREAD EXTENDED

USING MAJOR & MINOR ARCANA

This spread is based on one of the best-known Tarot spreads. It uses the Major and Minor Arcana cards and gives approximately a six-month reading.

This spread can be used for a general reading, or it can be used to gain insight and answers to a specific area of your life that needs guidance.

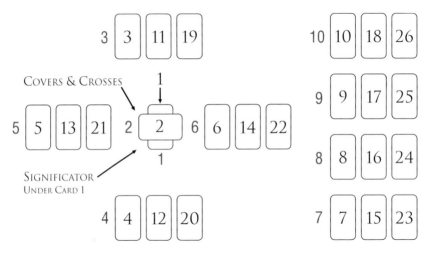

INTERPRETING THE CELTIC CROSS SPREAD

1 Covers the significator, which represents the person you are doing the reading for.

2 Crosses the significator (directly crosses him).

3 Crowns him (on top of him).

4 Below him (influences leaving his life or the next situation to happen).

5 Behind him (influences leaving his life or the next situation to happen).

6 Before or in front of him (the next influence or situation to come into his life).

7 Himself (this is personally around the significator).

8 Home/work.

9 His hopes or worst fear – which may be holding him back in life.

10 The outcome of the reading.

A Sample Reading

Bob is our significator. He is over 25 years old with red hair and hazel eyes.

Significator – King of Wands.

Bob's Celtic Cross Reading With Minor Arcana Only

KING OF WANDS
*Man over 25 years.
Green eyes, blonde to red hair.
Restless, outspoken, ambitious.*

Significator

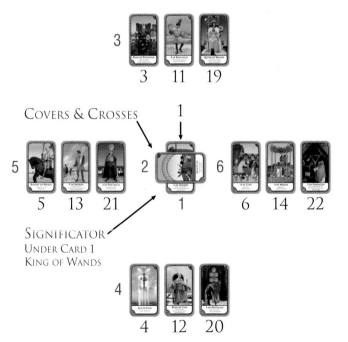

Covers & Crosses

Significator
Under Card 1
King of Wands

3   3 11 19

1

5 5 13 21   2 1 6 6 14 22

4 4 12 20

10 10 18 26

9 9 17 25

8 8 16 24

7 7 15 23

CELTIC CROSS SPREAD EXTENDED *(continued)*

1&2 CARDS 1 & 2 COVERING & CROSSING BOB

6 of Swords & 10 of Cups
Bob is turning his boat out of troubled waters. Better days ahead which could lead to a celebration very soon.

3 CARDS 3–11–19 CROWNING BOB

King of Pentacles–2 of Pentacles–Queen of Wands
Our professional businessman, with dark hair, is really juggling a number of issues in his life at the moment, connected to a fiery, outspoken woman, with red or blonde hair. This woman approaches her life with a positive outlook and together they can find an acceptable outcome to the issues at hand.

4 CARDS 4–12–20 BELOW BOB

Ace of Cups–King of Cups–5 of Pentacles
Offer of a helping hand coming from a soft, gentle man with blonde or light brown hair and blue or grey eyes. There have been a lot delays in Bob's life, but he feels now is the time to move forward with confidence as he comes in from the cold, and the money starts to flow for his future.

5 Cards 5–13–21 Behind Bob

Knight of Wands–5 of Swords–4 of Pentacles

An important letter is coming to Bob that will contain some negative news, but when Bob explores the contents of the letter fully he realises this gives him the upper hand on a number of points raised in the letter or document. The end result will bring money improvements in his life, but he may need to spend some money in order to gain more in the long run.

6 Cards 6–14–22 Before Bob

6 of Cups–4 of Wands–3 of Pentacles

There have been a lot of money fluctuations in Bob's life. Bob has been made an offer, which he feels he will turn down, in relation to a house or property in a country setting. There may need to be some negotiation here and he will then see major improvements underway. However, there may still be some delays in the early stages of the negotiations.

7 Cards 7–15–23 Yourself
(Bob the Significator)

3 of Cups–5 of Cups–8 of Cups

Bob is celebrating the end of his negotiations over the house and money matters he was previously experiencing. There have been a number of emotional and financial losses connected to the negotiations. Bob is now able turn his back and walk away from all of these situations, towards a positive future.

CELTIC CROSS SPREAD EXTENDED *(continued)*

8 CARDS 8–16–24
HOUSE/WORK FOR BOB

9 of Wands–8 of Swords–Ace of Wands

Bob really needs to take a step out of the situation to clearly see what the next moves may be in his professional and personal life. The pressure from both areas have caused him to feel very bound and gagged, which, no doubt, has blocked his energy. He is now able to walk away from this to a new beginning with a lot of new opportunities for the future.

9 CARDS 9–17–25
HOPES & FEARS FOR BOB

9 of Cups–Knight of Swords–10 of Wands

Bob is feeling that improvements are certainly under way in his life. He is charging forward to resolve all the obstacles that are weighing him down. There will be a speedy finish to the matters at hand.

10 CARDS 10–18–26
OUTCOME FOR BOB

2 of Cups–Queen of Cups–Ace of Swords

Bob has peace of mind that his life is certainly improving. He has now commenced the journey of life with a soft, gentle female with blonde/brown hair and blue eyes, who is helping him leave behind the frustrations and money losses of the past and look towards a positive new future.

BOB'S CELTIC CROSS READING WITH MAJOR & MINOR ARCANA

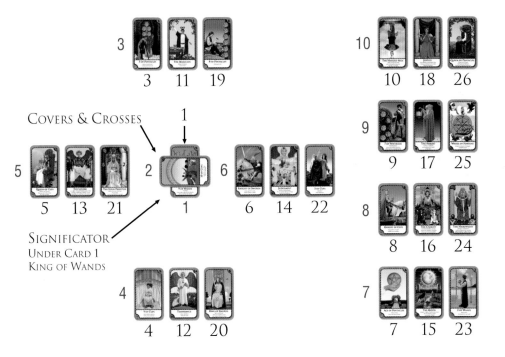

COVERS & CROSSES

SIGNIFICATOR
UNDER CARD 1
KING OF WANDS

3   3   11   19

1

2   1   6   14   22

5   13   21

4   12   20

10   18   26

9   17   25

8   16   24

7   15   23

CELTIC CROSS SPREAD EXTENDED *(continued)*

1&2 CARDS 1&2 COVERS & CROSSES BOB

9 of Wands–10 of Cups

Bob is very undecided about his next move. He needs to take a step out of the situation so he can see it more clearly. The decisions he has made have been clear and decisive, which will lead to celebrations in his life.

3 CARDS 3–11–19 CROWNING BOB

5 of Pentacles–The Magician–8 of Pentacles

Bob is experiencing some delays around money at the present time. Nothing is fixed in his life at the moment. The Magician card indicates the element of surprise, so he will need to be ready to make changes and decisions quickly. In the midst of the changes in Bob's personal and professional life there will be increased duties and more work coming his way.

4 CARDS 4–12–20 BELOW BOB

9 of Cups–Temperance–King of Swords

Bob feels there is excitement in the air with improvements under way in all areas of his life. There have been some testing times with money and financial matters that needed attention and careful handling – especially with important matters connected to a man with brown/grey hair and deep hazel/brown eyes. This man could be very cold and abrasive in his mannerisms, commands respect from those around him, and at times has a very arrogant.

5 CARDS 5–13–21 BEHIND BOB

Queen of Cups–The Lovers–The High Priestess

Bob has been fortunate to have a blonde/brown haired, blue eyed lady friend in his life, who has been gentle in her approach to helping him through the issues faced in his professional and personal life. This is now leading Bob to look towards her in a different light, as over time he has slowly been falling in love with her. He feels there have been a lot of secret agendas in their lives which have been revealed over a period of time in their friendship. Bob feels there may be a higher force at work to bring this union together for purposes yet to be revealed. With the influence of the highest card, it will be a match made in heaven.

6 CARDS 6–14–22 BEFORE BOB

Knight of Swords–Judgement–3 of Wands

Bob is charging forward with great speed. The decisions he is making are final and the only decisions that can be made under the circumstances. Bob is now spending time surveying his kingdom for the future and what lies ahead.

7 CARDS 7–15–23 YOURSELF
(BOB THE SIGNIFICATOR)

Ace of Pentacles–The Moon–2 of Wands

Money is coming. Bob's divine wish is being granted. There has been a lot of deception around emotional issues connected with his personal and professional life, which has left him feeling very drained. He needs to take a short journey to recharge his batteries.

 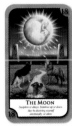 

CELTIC CROSS SPREAD EXTENDED *(continued)*

8 CARDS 8–16–24
HOME/WORK FOR BOB

Knight of Cups–The Chariot–The Hierophant
Bob will receive a message or letter that will enable him to be victorious over very important matters regarding his professional and personal life that have been taking a long. These matters will now be resolved quickly in Bob's favour, and he will need to sign some official documents to bring final closure.

9 CARDS 9–17–25
HOPE/FEAR FOR BOB

7 of Pentacles–The Hermit–Wheel of Fortune
Bob has experienced a number of frustrations around his professional and personal life. There was a period of loneliness and soul-searching about what was the right decision to act on next. After a period of contemplation the future looks very bright. With The Wheel of Fortune turning in his favour and with an increase in money, his old way of life finally comes to a close and a new direction is being cast.

10 CARDS 10–18–26
OUTCOME FOR BOB

The Hanged Man–Justice–Queen of Pentacles
Bob is getting stronger with each passing day. After a lot of deliberating and delaying about his future, he can now proceed with great determination. There is a legal situation that has to be resolved and will involve important documents and legal papers. Bob will engage the services of a professional, dark haired woman who is very businesslike and can be domineering in her approach to get the results that she requires. She will bring about the truth in the above matters, and finally bring justice and balance into Bob's life at every level.

Daily Inspiration Spread

Using Major & Minor Arcana

This is a quick spread that will provide a reading for the next couple of days or weeks.

1 Shuffle the cards.

2 Take 9 cards from the top of the deck.

3 Read the first row, from left to right (1–2–3 cards).

4 Read the second row, from left to right (4–5–6 cards).

5 Then read the third row, from left to right (7–8–9 cards).

6 Read each row vertically (1–4–7 cards, 2–5–8 cards, 3–6–9 cards).

7 Read in a diagonal line, from top left to bottom right (1–5–9 cards).

8 Then read in a diagonal line, from top right to bottom left (3–5–7 cards).

9 The most important card is No. 5, in the middle of the spread. This becomes the now card.

A Sample Reading

Mary's Daily Inspiration Reading

1   7 of Swords, Ace of Cups, Page of Wands

2   Ace of Wands, Page of Pentacles, Page of Swords

3   7 of Wands, 8 of Pentacles, The Devil

Horizontal

Mary's hopes and wishes are coming true. She has drawn the highest card in the Minor Arcana. This leads her to emotional security for an important journey she needs to take. The birth of new ideas and creative thinking will lead her to new opportunities that were only pipe-dreams before. Mary will have to learn some new skills. She needs to stop looking back over her shoulder in to the past and focus on the future. Mary is now able to overcome her frustrations of the past and move forward. There is a lot of work ahead of her and she will be able to break the chains that have been holding her back.

Vertical

Mary's hopes and wishes are coming true with the birth of new ideas, and creative thinking will lead her to new opportunities that were only pipe-dreams before. She will need to learn some new skills. Mary is able to overcome her problems with the help of friends giving her the emotional support and security she needs. She will need to learn some new work skills. This will lead her to a lot more travel connected with her profession. Mary needs to stop looking back over her past and break free from those chains that were holding her back.

Diagonal

Mary's wishes are coming true at great speed. Her determination to learn work skills will help break the chains of the past quicker. This will lead to more exciting opportunities to travel, with her profession always leading her into new and exciting experiences which give her greater skills to overcome the past.

The Now Card

Mary has to learn some new skills and this will enrich and deepen her life.

GLOSSARY

COURT CARDS   Page, Knight, Queen and King cards in the Minor Arcana.

DECK   Pack or set of cards.

MAJOR ARCANA   The 22 cards of the original Tarot.

MINOR ARCANA   The 56 cards added to the original Tarot cards, including
                     the four different houses or suits – Cups, Wands, Swords
                     and Pentacles.

QUERENT   The person who is having the reading, or asking the
                     question (see significator).

SIGNIFICATOR   The person who is having the reading. Sometimes known
                     as the querent. The card chosen to represent this person is
                     also known as the significator. This is based on sex, age
                     and hair and eye colouring.

SPREAD   Name given to the various ways in which cards must be
                     laid out for a reading, for example, the Celtic Cross Spread.

CONCLUSION

I've been asked many times what makes a good Tarot reader. I can only conclude
that you need to believe in the knowledge that is being shared with you, and
that you should always keep an open mind and remember we all have free will.
Life is a journey of learning, sharing and discovery, which leads us to our destiny.

I know you will always be amazed by the information given to you by the Tarot
cards. Remember that practise makes perfect. As time goes on, you will find your
own unique way of interpreting the cards. Let your intuition develop at its own pace,
don't force it. I believe we never stop learning in our lives, so continue to read any
information you can about the Tarot because some of this information may be useful
to you. Each teacher of Tarot uses different methods and slightly different
interpretations. I always suggest to my students that if you like it and it works for
you, then adopt it. If not, then let go.

You will find the more you work with the cards, the more enlightened and enriched
your life will become. Enjoy the ancient knowledge and wisdom that is there for all
of us to share.

ABOUT THE AUTHOR

AMANDA HALL is a clairvoyant astrologer, who started reading the Tarot when she was very young. Amanda designed a Tarot course for the general public in the early 1980s, and was the first lecturer to teach a higher education Tarot course at Gold Coast TAFE college in 1992. She has also taught by correspondence for over 20 years. Amanda spent three years touring Australia with one of the country's largest exhibition companies, performing readings, lecturing and conducting workshops in the psychic arena. Her work included television interviews, talk-back radio and regular newspaper columns. Amanda now resides on the Gold Coast with her partner Jack Egerton, where they operate and own Golden Tree Productions. Amanda reads for the public, writes books and articles and gives interviews and lectures around Australia. Amanda assists Jack with the production of TV commercials, documentaries and all facets of video production and multimedia.

The *Simply Tarot* project is dedicated to two special men in my life, my late husband Peter James Hall and my colleague (the late) Marc De-Pascale. Without their support and encouragement from the beginning of my own journey with Tarot, and over many years, this project would not have been possible. From the bottom of my heart, I thank the two very special gentlemen who would be smiling from above.